BEST HIKING TRAILS
in Western Newfoundland

BEST HIKING TRAILS
in Western Newfoundland

for Novice to Expert

KEITH NICOL

BREAKWATER

©1987 Keith Nicol

Canadian Cataloguing in Publication Data

Nicol, Keith
    Best hiking trails in western Newfoundland: for novice to expert
    ISBN 0-920911-35-8

    1. Hiking – Newfoundland – Guide-books. 2. Trails – Newfoundland – Guide-books. 3. Newfoundland – Description and travel – 1981   - Guide-books. I. Title.
    GV199.44.C32N48 1987   917.18'044   C87-094533-5

Cover: Table Mountain, near Port aux Basques, with the Gulf of St. Lawrence in the background. Photography by Keith Nicol.

Maps by Sam Crowley, Peregrine Corporation.

The Publisher gratefully acknowledges the support of The Canada Council.

CAUTION

List of Trails

Introduction

This guidebook, intended for anyone interested in hiking in Western Newfoundland, is designed to highlight spectacular coastlines and mountain vistas that many visitors and Newfoundlanders might never otherwise see. Newfoundland has few developed trails built specifically for hiking. However, numerous 'trails' do exist; trails that may have initially been used to connect communities prior to road construction, trails to gain access to areas for berry picking, trails which local residents have used for decades. These trails are accurately depicted on the maps in this guidebook, but in many cases it is suggested that actual topographic maps be obtained to aid the hiker. This is particularly true for hikes leading into the Long Range Mountains.

Short sections on human settlement and natural history, map reading and suggested equipment and clothing are presented as an aid to your enjoyment of hiking.

Western Newfoundland has numerous features which make it some of the best hiking in Eastern North America. The Long Range Mountains, home to a variety of wildlife (including moose, ptarmigan, arctic and snowshoe hare and caribou), extend five hundred kilometres from Port aux Basques to St. Anthony. Glaciation has sculpted and eroded these mountain slopes, creating a very scenic and rugged landscape.

Roughly half of the hikes outlined in this guidebook illustrate various access routes into the Long Range Mountains. Frequently the mountain summits are barren or are covered in tundra-like vegetation, allowing these hikes to be extended further. However, since these routes are more difficult than the coastal hikes they are presented with the more experienced hiker in mind.

Newfoundland's coastline is tremendously varied, ranging from long sandy beaches to spectacular cliffs, and provides the opportunity for frequent encounters with interesting colonies of shore birds, and possibly whale sightings just offshore. The remaining hikes, therefore, focus on coastal trails or short trails to local points of interest. These hikes are easier and are generally suited to people of all ages. It should be noted, however, that since these trails are *not* formally marked and maintained the trail descriptions presented here are valid at the time of publication but may change over time. Since local people often walk these trails, stop and ask if you are unsure where a trail starts;

7

Newfoundlanders are well-known for their friendliness and hospitality and will be happy to be of assistance.

Several of the trails given in this book are within the boundaries of the province's provincial parks. It should be noted that a user fee — seasonal, daily entry, or camping — is charged to visitors (with the exception of senior citizens resident in the province) using the facilities of any of these parks. Information on, and the payment of, fees can be obtained at the entry station of any provincial park.

Hiking is a superb way to see a landscape. It costs little and requires few skills. Walking not only stimulates our muscles, but provides psychological benefits as well. As we become more urbanized, our wilderness becomes more valuable, offering opportunities for adventure, nature appreciation, contemplation and reflection. It is hoped that these hikes help you enjoy Newfoundland's outdoors.

Settlement History of Western Newfoundland

Western Newfoundland, permanently settled at a later date than the eastern portion of the province, has a remarkable history of settlement, in great measure owing to the varied backgrounds of its pioneers. Newfoundland's west coast was first explored by Vikings roughly one thousand years ago. Based on archaeological work initiated by Helge Ingstad in 1960, Parks Canada has recreated a Viking settlement at L'Anse aux Meadows, just north of St. Anthony. How long this site was originally occupied is unknown, but apparently it was sufficient to build substantial houses and a 'smithy' for forging iron tools.

The next documented European contact was probably that of Jacques Cartier in 1537. He sailed past Pointe Riche (near Port aux Choix on the Northern Peninsula) and anchored at Cow Head (near Gros Morne National Park). Cartier subsequently sailed past the Bay of Islands, explored the Port au Port Peninsula, and then sailed southward to Cape Anguille. From there his vessels turned westward into the Gulf of St. Lawrence and he returned to France via the Strait of Belle Isle.

Although Western Newfoundland has this history of early exploration by Europeans, permanent settlement didn't occur until the late 1700s and early 1800s. Even then, the Treaty of Versailles in 1783, which gave France the right to fish and dry their catch on Newfoundland's west coast, greatly affected the rate of settlement over the next 120 years. Frequent disputes over the issue of permanent settlement between the French and the English slowed the growth of this area, and as a result much of Western Newfoundland didn't really begin to develop until the mid 1800s and later. In fact, it wasn't until

1904, when France gave up her claims in exchange for a territory in West Africa, that the issue was officially settled. However, the French legacy remains: many of today's place names (Port aux Basques, Port au Port, Port aux Choix, to name a few) date from their earlier fishing rights. Aside from the French and English, other ethnic groups — including Acadian, Irish, Scottish, Channel Islanders, and Micmac Indians — settled Western Newfoundland. Today, the major centres are Port aux Basques, Stephenville, Corner Brook and St. Anthony. With a population of 25,000 Corner Brook is the largest community on the west coast and ranks as the province's second largest city.

Geology

One of the attractions of hiking in Western Newfoundland is the rock assemblages, which are some of the most spectacular in Eastern Canada. In fact, Western Newfoundland has been called the "eighth wonder of the world." To appreciate this geology, the hiker should be aware of some of the basic concepts of plate tectonics. This relatively recent theory in the earth sciences states that the earth is composed of ten to twelve large *plates* which often include both continent and ocean. These plates are many kilometres thick and float like a raft on the plastic-like inner mantle of the earth. Due to the heat released by radioactive decay within the earth, this plastic-like layer slowly convects, like a thick soup simmering on the stove. The convection currents push the *rafts* or plates apart in some places, in the process causing earthquakes and undersea lava flows. Where plates collide, buckling and uplifting frequently occur creating many of the world's mountain ranges. Today there are well defined global belts of volcanic activity, mountain building, and earthquakes thought to be due to these plate movements.

Although Western Newfoundland is not *now* at a plate boundary, there is very good evidence to suggest that it once was quite active geologically. Because of the great variety of rock types to be found in Newfoundland it appears that the continents of North America and Africa collided roughly five hundred million years ago. This collision caused volcanic activity and uplifted other rocks to create the Long Range Mountains. The plates then separated (roughly two hundred million years ago) and a new land was created — Newfoundland, partly North American (along the west coast) and partly African (on the Avalon Peninsula), with crumpled sea floor in between (making up Central Newfoundland).

One of the most interesting types of bedrock found in Western Newfoundland is *peridotite*. This rock has its origins from several kilometres below the ocean floor and is now found *atop* portions of the Long Range Mountains, pushed to this position when North America and Africa "collided." What makes periodotite so unusual is its toxic influence on most vegetation. Where peridotite outcrops — in the Blomidon Mountains (near Corner Brook), on the North Arm Mountains, and near Trout River in Gros Morne National Park — this brownish rock stands in stark contrast to the green vegetation found on the surrounding bedrock. Keep your eye out for this rare and distinctive rock.

Subsequent glacial activity has further eroded and steepened many of the slopes of the Long Range Mountains. The fjords of the Bay of Islands and Bonne Bay were formed this way, but the most spectacular examples are found in Gros Morne National Park. Ten Mile Pond, Baker's Brook Pond, and Western Brook Pond are all dramatic steep-walled glacial valleys. Although it is tempting to speculate that the flat-top nature of the Long Range Mountains is due to previous glacial erosion, it is more likely that the colliding plates pushed up relatively flat land and that this has resulted in the plateau-like features of the mountain range.

Hiking is the most appropriate way to explore Newfoundland's diverse geologic history. So when you see fossils, flat-topped tablelands, or sheer walled valleys, consider the complex geologic changes that have occurred on this Island. In this light, Western Newfoundland truly is the "eighth wonder of the world."

Flora and Fauna of Western Newfoundland

Flora

Much of Western Newfoundland lies in boreal forest, a type of forest which spreads across much of sub-arctic Canada. The main tree types are black spruce (*Picea mariana*), balsam fir (*Abies balsamea*), white spruce (*Picea glauca*), and white birch (*Betula papyrifera*). In wind-swept areas these trees often take on a stunted and contorted form. While the correct name for this vegetation form is *krummholz* (a German word meaning 'bent stick'), in Newfoundland *tuckamore* is used to describe this almost inpenetrable mass of branches and needles. Generally, when encountering tuckamore the wise hiker will look for game trails through it rather than plunge through with no trail. In more poorly drained sites (at lower elevations), larch (*Larix laricina*), one of the few coniferous trees which drop their needles in the fall, may be found in conjunction with other bog plants.

One of the most interesting bog plants is the carnivorous pitcher plant (*Sarracenia purpurea*), Newfoundland's provincial flower. The pitcher plant manufactures a sweet perfume which attracts insects. Many fine slippery hairs form within the *pitchers* and insects slip down these hairs to become trapped. Enzymes produced by the plant dissolve the insect and the plant obtains nutrients not available in the acid soil in which it grows. Although many people think that the pitcher plant is found only in Newfoundland, it actually has a very wide range, extending to Florida in the south and British Columbia in the west. Another bog plant worth looking for is the cloudberry (*Rubus chamaemorus*), known locally as the bakeapple. This delicate berry is often gathered by local people in the late summer or early fall for preserves, pies and tarts. Other more common berries which grow at lower elevations include wild strawberries, raspberries, and blueberries, with the latter frequently very abundant.

Pitcher Plant

At higher altitudes and in wind-swept areas along the coast tundra or barren ground vegetation is found. For survival, plants in these environments take on a dwarf or cushion-like appearance. Lichens (*Cladina alpestris*, et cetera), mosses (*Rhacomstrium lanuginosum*), and dwarf willows (*Salix arctica*) and birches (*Betula papyrifera*) frequent this zone. As well, insect-eating sundews (*Drosera rotundifolia*) and butterworts (*Pinguicula*) can be found in many tundra and lowland environments.

Generally, the nature of the underlying bedrock seems to have a minimal impact on vegetation in most of Newfoundland. However, a striking exception occurs where peridotite is found at the earth's surface.

This bedrock has low levels of calcium and high concentrations of chromium, nickel and magnesium which are probably toxic to most plants. The weathering of peridotite produces a highly alkaline soil which is also a restrictive factor, resulting in a vegetation-free landscape in remarkable contrast to adjacent forested slopes. Despite the general lack of vegetation some plants, including the pitcher plant, larch and the common juniper (*Juniperus communis*), have adapted to the unusual chemistry of peridotite.

Fauna

Because Newfoundland is an island numerous animals common to Nova Scotia and Labrador are not found here. In fact, only fourteen indigenous species of mammals are found on the island. These include the beaver (*Castar canadensis caecator*), red fox (*Vulpes vulpes deletrix*), black bear (*Ursus americanus hamiltoni*), arctic hare (*Lepus arctica bangsii*) and caribou (*Rangifer tarandus terraneovae*). Moose (*Alces alces*) were introduced in 1878 and now number over 40,000 animals.

No indigenous amphibians or reptiles are found on the island, so there is no need to worry about snakes while hiking through tall grass or on rocky slopes.

In contrast to mammals and reptiles, Newfoundland has a large and varied bird population, with 227 species of birds recorded. Of particular interest are the fish-catching osprey (*Pandion haliaetus*), bald eagle (*Haliaetus lencocephalus*), willow ptarmigan (*Lagopus lagopus*), as well as the more common herring gull (*Larus argentatus*) and black-capped chickadee (*Parus atricapillus*).

Clothing and Equipment

Hiking normally requires very little special clothing or equipment. The most important requirement is choosing appropriate footwear. For many of the shorter hikes in this book running or tennis shoes are adequate; for some of the longer hikes, however, choosing appropriate footwear is a challenge since on any given day a backpacker might encounter loose rock, dry alpine meadows, and wet sedge or moss covered bogs. Although standard leather hiking boots are preferred for the rock and dry meadows, they inevitably get wet when crossing low lying areas. Therefore the traditional rubber boot used by the local fisherman is a more useful choice to ensure dry feet. They are inexpensive and, despite first impressions, comfortable to walk in.

Dressing for a hike may also require planning. You will often encounter different climatic regimes and your own body heat production needs to be considered. At first you may be chilly, then after a few moments the sweat may be poring from your brow; when you stop to rest the wind that was refreshing while climbing is now uncomfortablely cool. The solution is to dress in layers, adjusting your clothing to match your exertion and the prevailing weather. It is essential to bring a waterproof windbreaker (and possibly rain pants) for longer hikes and an extra sweater is often recommended. Since tight fitting pants will bind as you lift your legs, it is best to wear a loose fitting pair if the hike involves very much elevation gain. In cooler weather a toque and gloves may be appropriate.

It is frequently a good idea for one or more members of a hiking group to carry a small pack. A small day pack is often sufficient, but choose one with padded shoulder straps and a waist strap if possible. Include the following basic equipment for a day long hike.

Checklist

- anorak (waterproof or highly water resistant)
- extra sweater
- extra socks
- lunch and snacks
- map
- compass
- candle
- matches or lighter
- knife
- water bottle

- possibly rain pants
- toilet paper
- camera and film

- insect repellant
- sunscreen
- aspirin
- moleskin (for blisters)
- bandaids
- gauze dressings
- antiseptic cream

Map Reading

Although the maps included in this book are suitable for most hikes, for others it is best to obtain and know how to read actual topographic maps. Think of a map as a puzzle: the more you can interpret the map, the more information it will present to you. A map of a flat landscape is easy to understand. By orienting the map toward north, objects are in their correct geographic location and the distance to points of interest can be easily determined by the map scale. As the terrain becomes more varied, so the map reading becomes more complex and requires more skill.

All topographic maps use contours to illustrate elevation; contours connect points of equal elevation. All topographic maps have a constant contour interval which is usually marked at the bottom of the map. In Western Newfoundland the typical contour interval on topographic maps is fifty feet. However, in order to simplify the landscape we have used a contour interval of 250 feet on most maps reproduced in this book. Because of this simplification, it is suggested that actual topographic maps be obtained for the more mountainous hikes (and their extensions) presented in this guide.

It is important that those using topographic maps recognize how basic landforms are illustrated. When streams or rivers are crossed, contours will v upstream — hence that is how valleys are presented on *topo* maps. Ridges are often good viewpoints or lookouts, and contours v downhill in these instances. When contour lines are close together, the terrain is steep; widely spaced contour lines indicate a more gently sloping landscape.

As a safety precaution — to guard against such possibilities as losing the trail or the occurrence of fog — a compass should be carried on longer hikes. A compass can also be used to orient a map, thereby allowing you to easily identify landmarks. Since maps are oriented toward true north, and a compass points to magnetic north, a correction known as magnetic declination needs to be applied. In Western Newfoundland magnetic declination varies between 25°W at Port aux Basques to 31°W in the St. Anthony area.

To orient your map with a compass follow this procedure:

(a) Start by placing the compass along the *magnetic north line* of the declination diagram (usually found along the right margin of topographic maps). Set the compass to 360°.

(b) Turn the map, with compass lying on it, until the magnetic north needle points to the north symbol in the compass housing.

The map is now oriented and objects on the map are in their correct geographic position.

Topographic maps can be ordered from the Department of Energy, Mines and Resources, 615 Booth Street, Ottawa, Ontario K1A 0E9, or can be purchased from Barnes Sporting Goods in Corner Brook, the Visitor's Centre in Gros Morne National Park, as well as other locations.

Hazards to Hikers

Animals

Fortunately Western Newfoundland has few hazards for which one can't prepare or plan. There are no grizzly bears, but black bears are found in many areas. Count yourself lucky if you should see one as they will generally be the first to move if they hear you approaching. Bears, however, are unpredictable, so never approach one to get a better view or a closeup photograph. Should you come face to face with a bear, don't run but walk slowly backward and try not to panic.

Moose, particularly a cow with a calf, are probably more of a hazard to hikers than black bears. This is particularly true in the early summer when the calves are smaller and their mothers more protective. Again, don't approach a moose for a closeup photograph; use a telephoto lens and keep your distance. Normally caribou are not a hazard, but should not be approached too closely.

Mosquitoes and blackflies are not always present but be prepared for them, especially on hikes into the Long Range Mountains. Usually wind will minimize the bug problem, but it is best to pack insect repellant with you just in case. Long sleeves and pants will reduce the insect nuisance.

Weather

Weather hazards can usually be planned for if hikers watch the weather and obtain up-to-date forecasts prior to departing on a trip. Since many of the hikes in this book are not on formally marked trails, using visual clues to keep track of the route is essential. Therefore, don't start off some of the longer hikes if poor weather is forecast since fog can form quickly, especially in the mountains. Also, since temperatures drop and winds usually increase with elevation, dress and pack extra clothing accordingly.

If some one in your party does get chilled, watch for the symptoms of *hypothermia*. Hyopthermia is probably a hiker's most serious hazard, and contrary to popular opinion doesn't only occur in winter. In fact, hypothermia most often occurs in windy, wet conditions with temperatures between 1°-10°C (34°-50°F). The best way to avoid hypothermia is to bring extra clothing, especially a good rainsuit, wool hat, and mittens if poor weather is expected.

The key sympotms of hypothermia are uncontrollable shivering, stumbling, drowsiness, and an urge to rest and sleep. As hypothermia becomes more acute these symptoms may be accompanied by amnesia, irrational thought and slowed pulse and respiration rates. At this point immediate care is required since the victim is unable to produce sufficient heat to stop the body from cooling. Get the person out of cold and replace wet clothing with dry clothing. Put insulation under the victim's body. If a sleeping bag is available, have the victim get in the bag, preferably with another person. Give warm liquids and candy or sweetened foods. Resist the old wives' tale of giving alcohol since this only further cools the victim's body. Transport to medical care as soon as possible.

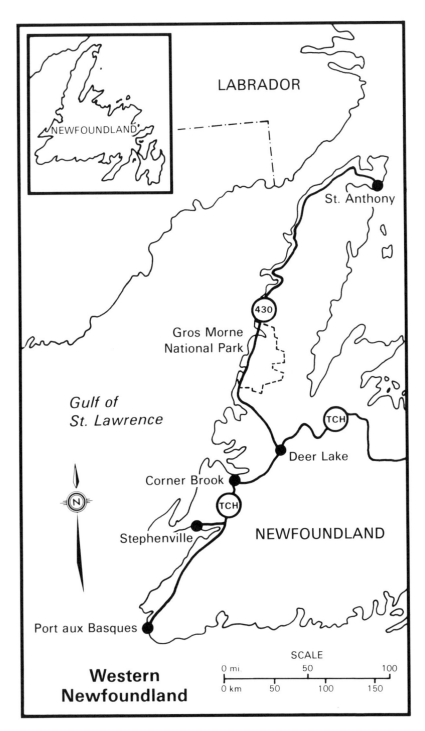

LABRADOR

St. Anthony

430

Gros Morne
National Park

Gulf of
St. Lawrence

TCH

Deer Lake

Corner Brook

TCH

Stephenville

NEWFOUNDLAND

Port aux Basques

**Western
Newfoundland**

NEWFOUNDLAND

SCALE

| 0 mi. | | 50 | | 100 |

| 0 km | 50 | 100 | 150 |

Hiking in the Port aux Basques Area

This southernmost part of Western Newfoundland is the main point of entry for visitors arriving from mainland Canada by ferry. As the name indicates, this gateway community was a port of call for Basque whalers, probably throughout the sixteenth century. In 1714 Micmac Indians were reported to have paddled across Cabot Strait from Cape Breton, Nova Scotia to the Port aux Basque area, and in 1871 the community was described as "the most westerly settlement of importance in Newfoundland...a place of considerable trade." In the early 1890s Port aux Basques was chosen as the western terminus of the Newfoundland railway, and by 1913 it was linked by gulf ferry service to the Canadian rail network.

The Port aux Basques-Codroy area has numerous hiking opportunities, from easy coastal walks to more strenuous treks into the Long Range Mountains. These mountains, which begin at Port aux Basques and extend five hundred kilometres in a northeasterly direction to St. Anthony, are geologically similar to the Appalachian Mountain chain which runs from Georgia to Maine in the United States. The Long Range Mountains are home to numerous small herds of caribou, moose, ptarmigan, and arctic hare. The caribou and arctic hare are of particular interest since they rarely occur in Southern Canada today.

Rose Blanche Lighthouse Trail

Location

Rose Blanche is located on highway 470, roughly 50 kilometres east of Port aux Basques. There are numerous small settlements enroute that are worth visiting either before or after a hike to the Rose Blanche Lighthouse. Isle aux Mort is particularly scenic; an astrolabe, a navigational instrument used by mariners in the fifteenth and sixteenth century, was found recently in the harbour of that community. Upon reaching Rose Blanche, turn left at the building which houses the town office, fire hall, and municipal garage. After descending a hill, turn left at a small pond and follow this road to the H & P Lounge. The unmarked trail starts between the houses next to the lounge (see map).

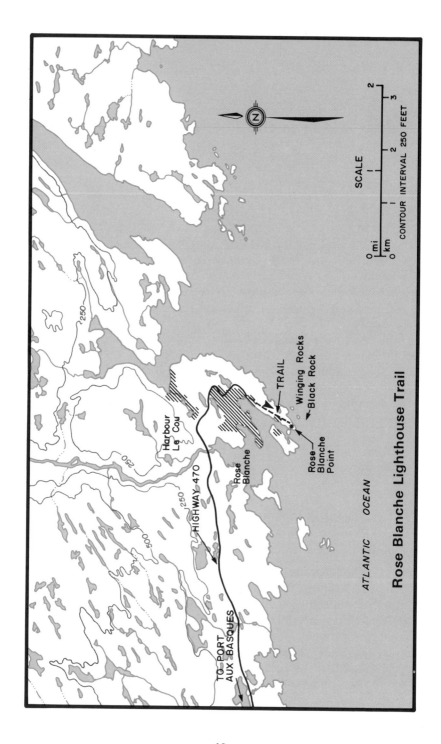

Rose Blanche Lighthouse Trail

Features

This short walk leads to an abandoned stone lighthouse. This lighthouse, built in 1856 from locally quarried granite, is surrounded by many interesting coves and the smoothy eroded bedrock shoreline is ideal for scrambling around.

Length

1 kilometre (one way)

Suitability

Since the trail is easy to follow and relatively flat, this is a good hike for families. Running or tennis shoes are the recommended footwear. Children will love clambering around on the rocky coastline, but use care if you try to climb up within the lighthouse. Remember it is not maintained, and has no handrails or guardrails on the spiral staircase leading to the top, so explore at your own risk.

Topographic Map Reference

Rose Blanche 10-0/10 (1:50,000)

Granite bedrock shoreline of the Rose Blanche Lighthouse Trail, with the lighthouse in the background.

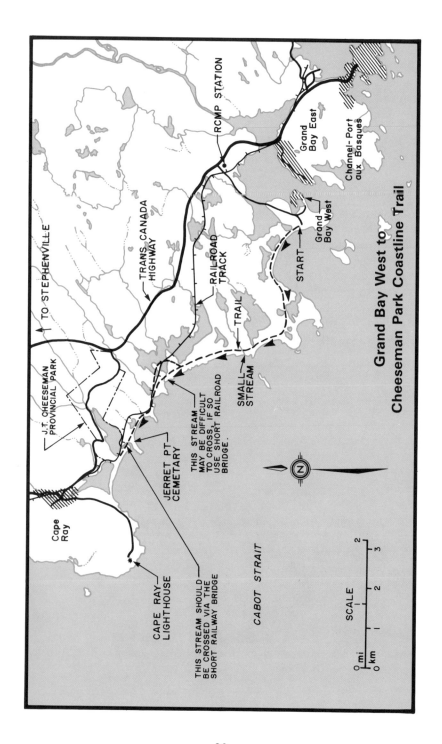

**Grand Bay West to
Cheeseman Park Coastline Trail**

RCMP STATION

Grand Bay East

Channel-Port
aux Basques

Grand
Bay West

START

TRANS CANADA
HIGHWAY

RAILROAD
TRACK

TRAIL

TO STEPHENVILLE

J.T. CHEESEMAN
PROVINCIAL PARK

SMALL
STREAM

THIS STREAM
MAY BE DIFFICULT
TO CROSS, IF SO
USE SHORT RAILROAD
BRIDGE.

JERRET PT
CEMETERY

Cape
Ray

N

CAPE RAY
LIGHTHOUSE

THIS STREAM SHOULD
BE CROSSED VIA THE
SHORT RAILWAY BRIDGE

CABOT STRAIT

SCALE

0 mi   1   2   3
0 km

Grand Bay West to Cheeseman Park Coastline Trail

Location

This unmarked coastal trail could start at either Grand Bay West or at Cheeseman Park, but starting at Grand Bay West (a 'suburb' of Port aux Basques) is recommended. Turn south at the RCMP building (on the Trans Canada Highway), drive to the beach at Grand Bay West, and follow the sandy beach to the right. Most of this route is on wide sandy beaches, with short trails cutting across the headlands. Use the short railroad bridges (shown on the map) to cross impassable coastal streams. The trip ends at Cheeseman Provincial Park.

Features

This is superb beach/headland route with well developed sand dunes in many places. Headlands are composed of interesting bedrock — sparkling mica schist in two sections. Throughout much of the hike the lighthouse at Cape Ray can be seen and the cemetary at Jerret Point is worth a visit. Numerous seabirds congregate along the many beaches which range in length from one-half to two kilometres in length — and most of the shore has beachcombing potential.

Length

10-11 kilometres (one way)

Suitability

This trip is recommended to anyone who wants to spend an afternoon walking along wide sandy beaches following seabirds or exploring rocky headlands. Because of the distance involved, families with young children may only want to explore a short portion of the trail. Since this route is unmarked pay close attention to the accompanying map and purchase a topographic map if possible. Traverse the short railroad bridges with care, and although trains are infrequent look both ways prior to crossing. Running or tennis shoes are the recommended footwear.

Topographic Map Reference

Port aux Basques 11-O/11 (1:50,000)

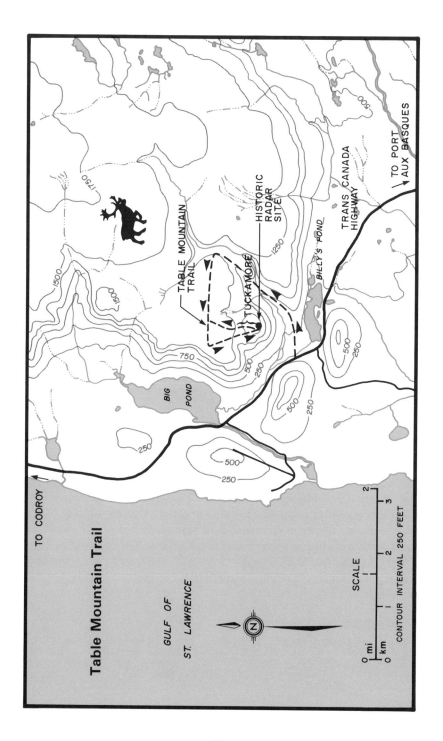

Table Mountain Trail

GULF OF
ST. LAWRENCE

TO CODROY

TO PORT
AUX BASQUES

TRANS CANADA
HIGHWAY

HISTORIC
RADAR
SITE

TUCKAMORE

TABLE MOUNTAIN
TRAIL

BILLY'S POND

BIG
POND

SCALE

0 mi
0 km

CONTOUR INTERVAL 250 FEET

N

1750
1500
1000
1250
750
500
250
900

 **Table Mountain Trail**

Location

Several kilometres west of Port aux Basques on the Trans Canada Highway is Table Mountain, used as a radar site during World War II. Access to the top can be gained by a gravel road which is closed to vehicular traffic by means of a locked gate. A sign reading "Table Mountain – Off Island – Digital Project" indicates the starting point. Follow this road to the tundra barrens on the top of Table Mountain.

Features

This route, climbing over 1300 feet, gives good views of Port aux Basques/Cape Ray to the south and the agricultural lands of the Codroy region to the north. The vegetation on top is tundra-like, making the route indicated on the map just one possibility. Although the "Off Island – Digital Project" tower is a visual drawback, the older remains of human occupation have historic interest. During World War II the Americans built a radar site, air strip, and assorted buildings on Table Mountain and the remnants of these features are worth investigating. Once to the north of the Digital Project tower and road, moose, caribou and ptarmigan sightings are possible.

Length

12 kilometres (return trip, following route outlined on map). Other routes are possible since much of the vegetation on top is tundra-like.

Suitability

The road is easy walking, but because it climbs over 1300 feet in elevation probably is not suitable for families with young children. The twelve kilometre loop described on the map can be done in running shoes, but once off the road heavier footwear is suggested. If you are ascending in questionable weather, stay close to the road or bring a map and compass since fog can form quickly and greatly reduce visibility. Bring a camera with lots of film: the views are spectacular!

Topographic Map Reference

Port aux Basques 11-0/11 (1:50,000)

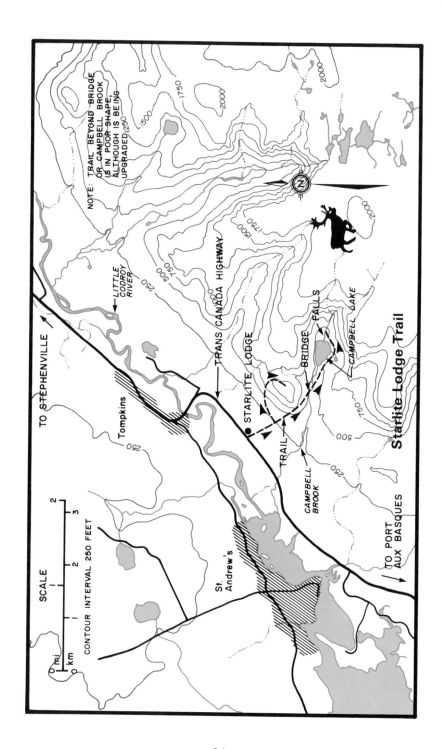

Starlite Lodge Trail

NOTE: TRAIL BEYOND BRIDGE OR CAMPBELL BROOK IS IN POOR SHAPE, ALTHOUGH IS BEING UPGRADED

TO STEPHENVILLE

LITTLE CODROY RIVER

Tompkins

TRANS CANADA HIGHWAY

STARLITE LODGE

BRIDGE

FALLS

CAMPBELL LAKE

TRAIL

CAMPBELL BROOK

TO PORT AUX BASQUES

St. Andrew's

SCALE

CONTOUR INTERVAL 250 FEET

 **Starlite Lodge Trail**

Location

Another access trail to the Long Range Mountains is behind the Starlite Lodge, located on the Trans Canada Highway just before the community of Tompkins. The trail is well maintained and easy to follow, although it ends shortly after it breaks out onto tundra vegetation. A side trail leads to Campbell Creek and a rough trail extends to Campbell Lake.

Features

The main route provides good access to the tundra and the top of the Long Range Mountains. Views to the west are of the agricultural lands of the Codroy and the Gulf of St. Lawrence, while those to the east, in complete contrast, are of steep rocky slopes, waterfalls and tundra stretching as far as the eye can see. Since the trail has numerous lookouts, benches, toilets and picnic tables at various locations enroute to the top, a family with young children could still go part way and enjoy this hike. The trail winds through nice stands of birch before breaking out into tundra.

Starlite Lodge Trail, with Campbell Lake in the background.

Length

2 kilometres (one way) to the top of the hill marked on the map. The trail to Campbell Creek would be 1.5 kilometres (one way), and an extra 1 kilometre takes the serious hiker to Campbell Lake. Note: the route beyond Campbell Lake is not in as good condition as the rest of the trail.

Suitability

This trail has lots to offer hikers of all ages. Because of the picnic tables and lookouts, a family with young children could enjoy this walk without reaching the top. For the serious backpaker, this trail provides good access to the extensive and the rarely-hiked expanses of the Long Range Mountains. For those venturing beyond the trail it is suggested that hikers be equipped with a map and compass and be familiar with wilderness route findings. Running shoes are adequate, but hikers planning to extend this trip will want heavier footwear.

Topographic Map Reference

Codroy 11-0/14 (1:50,000)

Hiking in the Stephenville Area

Located 166 kilometres from Port aux Basques, Stephenville was named
for Stephen LeBlanc, an early Acadian explorer, and settled in the mid
1840s. Because of its location between Europe and the United States,
it was chosen by the U.S. as the site of an air force base during World
War II. Much of the architectural heritage of Stephenville today dates
from this American influence. This area has spectacular coastal scenery,
and the Port aux Port Peninsula is one of the most ethnically diverse
regions of Newfoundland. The following hikes illustrate some of these
attributes.

 Sandy Point

Location

Sandy Point is in fact an island, once joined to the mainland at Flat
Bay several kilometres south of Stephenville Crossing. Access is via boat
from the community of St. Georges. In the past a local ferry service
has been operated by student job-creation projects but this service may
not exist from year to year. However, it is not difficult to arrange the
fifteen-minute boat ride to the island with a local resident. In the past
Louis Bennett of St. George's (phone 647-3963) has transported visitors
to the island for a nominal fee.

Features

Sandy Point was settled very early in the 1800s. In fact, at one time
it was the largest community on the entire west coast of Newfoundland
(by 1880 there were over one thousand residents). However, the
completion of the railroad through the adjacent settlement of St.
Georges in 1897 caused the considerable decline in population on
Sandy Point. With the provincial government resettling the remaining
population in the 1950s and '60s, the island lost its permanent residents.
Today only the concrete foundations of some of the larger buildings
remain. There are two cemetaries which are fascinating to investigate
since the headstones infer so much about origins of the early settlers.
In addition to the historic interest, Sandy Point has excellent beach

walking and interesting seabird populations. It is a nesting area of the piping plover and the European black headed gull. Foot paths criss-cross the area, and the beaches which ring the island are good for beach combing.

Sandy Point offers unlimited wilderness camping on grassy meadows for the explorer who wants to spend several relaxing days on the island. Although camping sites are numerous, to respect the beauty of this area it is suggested that hikers camp in areas that already have firepits and makeshift toilets. Sandy Point is a fragile area and care should be taken to ensure its landscape is preserved for hikers that follow you. Also, fresh water may be in short supply, so check into this before embarking on a multi-day trip.

Length

The map shows Sandy Point and one possible area for camping. Because hiking opportunities are just about unlimited, especially along the extensive beaches and numerous footpaths, no routes have been marked.

Suitability

This is an ideal place for family camping. It is a relaxing place to visit, and with a variety of natural and historic features to attract the inquisitive visitor, almost anyone would enjoy Sandy Point. Either bring water or ensure there is adequate water on the island for multi-day trips. Running shoes are generally suitable, but rubber boots may be required for walking on the trails that traverse near some of the small lakes or bogs.

Topographic Map Reference

Flat Bay 12B/7 (1:50,000)
Main Gut 12B/8 (1:50,000)

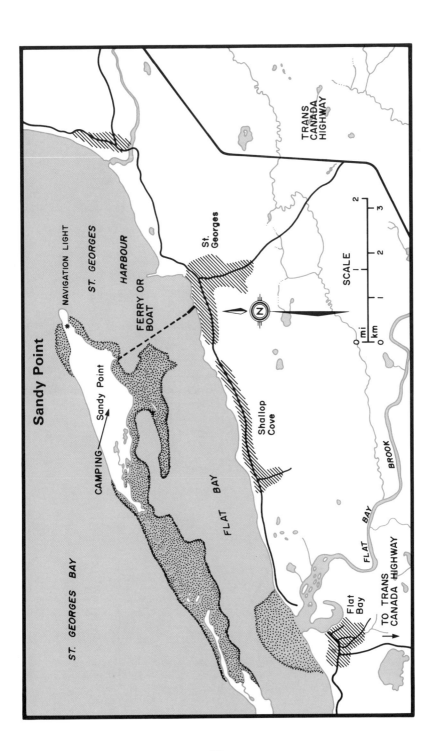

Sandy Point

ST. GEORGES BAY

NAVIGATION LIGHT

ST. GEORGES

HARBOUR

FERRY OR BOAT

CAMPING

Sandy Point

FLAT BAY

St. Georges

Shallop Cove

FLAT BAY

BROOK

Flat Bay

TO TRANS CANADA HIGHWAY

TRANS CANADA HIGHWAY

N

SCALE

mi
0   1   2
km
0   1   2   3

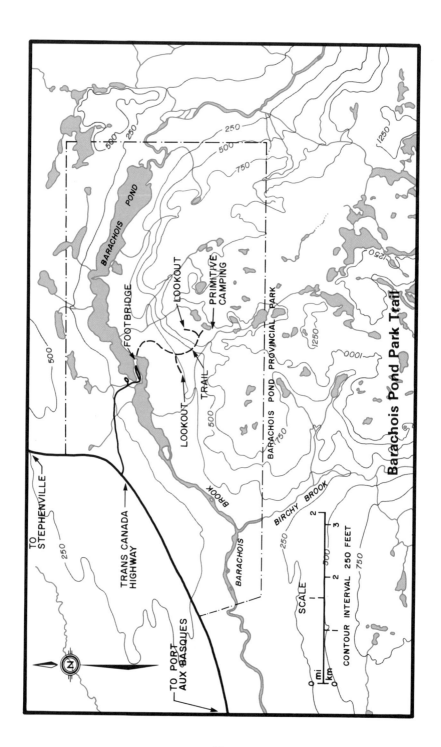

Barachois Pond Park Trail

TO STEPHENVILLE

TRANS CANADA HIGHWAY

TO PORT AUX BASQUES

BARACHOIS POND

FOOTBRIDGE

LOOKOUT

PRIMITIVE CAMPING

LOOKOUT TRAIL

BARACHOIS POND PROVINCIAL PARK

BARACHOIS BROOK

BIRCHY BROOK

SCALE

CONTOUR INTERVAL 250 FEET

30

 **Barachois Pond Park Trail**

Location

Barachois Pond Provincial Park is located just off the Trans Canada Highway, south of the Stephenville (highway 460) turnoff. A well-maintained hiking trail starts via a foot bridge at the end of one of the camping areas. Visitors to the Park are charged a small daily user fee.

Features

This trail winds through a variety of natural vegetation zones, including mixed forest, bog and subalpine environments, and climbs to the top of Erin Mountain. Although there is a lower elevation lookout point, the 1100 foot summit provides a spectacular view of St. George's Bay, Barachois Pond, and the Long Range Mountains. A primitive campsite exists for hikers wishing to camp near the summit. (Register at the park's entrance station if you intend to use this primitive camp site.)

Length

4.5 kilometres (one way)

Suitability

Although this trail climbs to over 1100 feet, it is well maintained and makes a good family hike. Since there is another lookout part of the way up the mountain, families with young children may want to do a shortened version. Parts of the trail near the summit are over rock and require care, so young children should not be allowed to run ahead in this area. Running shoes are adequate but light hiking boots are probably more suitable, especially for the rockier areas.

Topographic Map Reference

Main Gut 12B/8 (1:50,000)

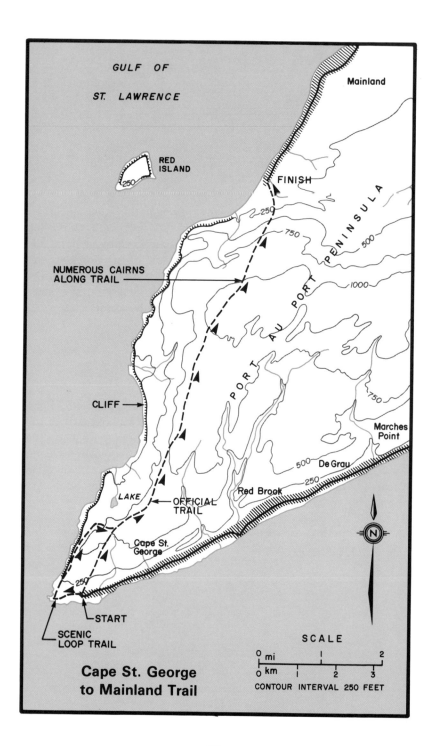

GULF OF

ST. LAWRENCE

Mainland

RED
ISLAND

250

FINISH

250

750

P E N I N S U L A

500

NUMEROUS CAIRNS
ALONG TRAIL

1000

P O R T   A U   P O R T

CLIFF

750

Marches
Point

LAKE

OFFICIAL
TRAIL

De Grau

500

250

Red Brook

Cape St.
George

N

250

START

SCENIC
LOOP TRAIL

Cape St. George
to Mainland Trail

SCALE

| 0 | mi | | 1 | | 2 |

| 0 | km | 1 | 2 | 3 |

CONTOUR INTERVAL 250 FEET

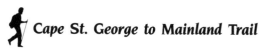# Cape St. George to Mainland Trail

Location

Cape St. George is located at the end of Highway 460 on the Port aux Port Peninsula. The French have had a profound influence in this part of Newfoundland and this region has been designated as Newfoundlnd's only bilingual district. The name of the nearby community of De Grau originates from the French phrase meaning "we are finished," referring to the completion of the summer fishery, and Marches Point was named for an early settler, John Marshe. Each August Cape St. George hosts a popular French folk festival. As well, for hikers in this area on June 24 (St. Jean Baptiste Day), you can join the residents of Mainland and Cape St. George as they walk the trail that connects their two communities. The trail starts near a red sign which says "Welcome to the Bill of the Cape." This is a good place to park your car. The unmarked trail starts opposite a green road sign which reads "Cape St. George," then passes by a beige building, and quickly becomes a well defined trail. If you start here, be sure to walk or drive the short distance to the end of the Cape since the sheer cliffs are certainly some of the most dramatic in Western Newfoundland. In fact, hikers equipped with a map and compass should walk along this spectacular coastline for approximately 2 kilometres. Just before the trail descends toward a small lake, cut across the sparsely vegetated barrens and pick up the main trail. Although this trail is illustrated on the map it is suggested that hikers use actual topographic maps to avoid missing this turn.

Features

Although the coastline along much of the Port aux Port area is scenic, the cliffs at Cape St. George are breathtaking. The combination of blue ocean, fishermen offshore in small dories, swooping gulls and sheer rock makes this one of the best coastal hikes in Newfoundland. Depending on the time of the year numerous wild flowers may be in bloom and we've noticed an unusually high population of marsh hawks along some sections. After the first leg the coastline becomes very rugged; this, combined with thick vegetation, dictates that the best route is about 1.5 kilometres inland. Much of the remainder of the trail (marked by cairns) follows a broad ridge to the community of Mainland. Red Island can be see just offshore for much of the trip. This island has historic significance since it was "considered by the French to be one of their best fishing stations on the West Coast." However, all of its inhabitants have moved or were resettled to the community of Mainland.

Length

11 kilometres (one way). If two vehicles are used, a one-way trip is possible, but otherwise a return via the same route is required.

Suitability

Because of the distances involved, this route is reserved for more experienced hikers. From past experience it is suggested that sufficient water or juice be taken since there are no places to obtain water along the way. Although it is tempting to use two cars and make this a one-way trip, the logistics should be examined since the distances are long and the trip very time consuming. Almost anyone can enjoy the hike to the cliffs at Cape St. George and spend a very pleasant afternoon exploring this spectacular area; however, use extreme care along the cliffs, especially with young children.

Topographic Map Reference

Mainland 12B/11 (1:50,000)
Cape St. George 12B/6 (1:50,000)

One of the breathtaking views to be seen along the Cape St. George to Mainland Trail.

Hiking in the Corner Brook Area

Numerous hiking possibilities exist in the Corner Brook area, some suitable for families but others, particularly those into the Blomidon Mountains, reserved for experienced backpakers. Glacial activity has produced dramatic coastlines and steep mountain slopes. The numerous islands dotting the bay — named the Bay of Islands by Captain James Cook in 1767 — make a very attractive backdrop for the hiker.

Roughly five kilometres east of Corner Brook is the small community of Steady Brook. Steady Brook is the ski capital of Newfoundland and a well-developed downhill skiing facility has been built on the slopes of Marble Mountain. There are two hiking possibilities here, one to a viewpoint overlooking Steady Brook Falls and another to the top of Marble Mountain.

 ## Steady Brook Falls Viewpoint

Location

Turn at the Marble Mountain Ski Area sign and follow the road behind the Petro Canada gas station. Follow this road a short distance, but do not cross the small bridge that crosses Steady Brook. Park in the rear parking lot of Marble Mountain near a road (marked with two red posts) which gradually starts to climb uphill. Follow this road for two hundred paces (from the red posts) until an unmarked trail branches to the left. This leads to the falls viewpoint.

Features

Excellent views of Steady Brook Falls which tumbles over one hundred feet. After a heavy rain, or in the spring of the year, this falls is spectacular.

Length

.5 kilometre (one way). From the viewpoint, another trail leads to the top of the falls.

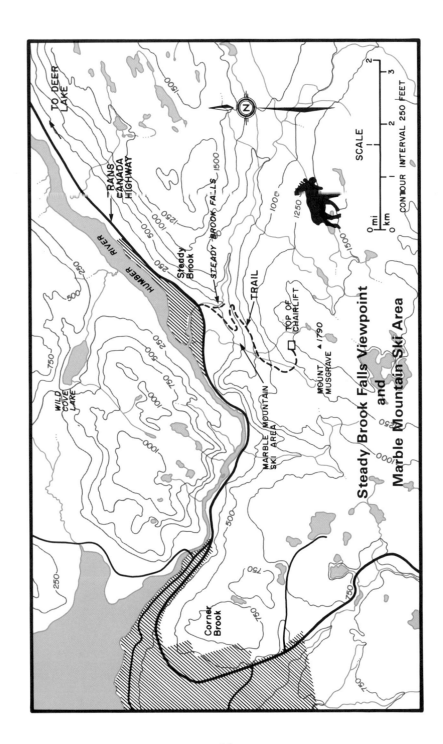

Steady Brook Falls Viewpoint
and
Marble Mountain Ski Area

TO DEER LAKE

TRANS CANADA HIGHWAY

HUMBER RIVER

Steady Brook

STEADY BROOK FALLS

TRAIL

TOP OF CHAIRLIFT

MOUNT MUSGRAVE ▲ 1790

MARBLE MOUNTAIN SKI AREA

WILD COVE LAKE

Corner Brook

SCALE

0 mi   2
0 km   1   2   3

CONTOUR INTERVAL 250 FEET

Suitability

Although this trail is great for families it is rocky is places and may be wet. Above the viewpoint it follows a ski run for part of the way and then an unmarked trail branches to the left. Follow this route to the top of the falls. Note: No fencing exists (at the time of this publication) at the viewpoint or beyond. For this reason, extreme care and caution is required both at the viewpoint and the trail beyond to the top of the falls, particularly with young children. Do not permit them to run ahead on this hike.

Topographic Map Reference

Corner Brook 12A/13 (1:50,000)

 Marble Mountain Ski Area

Location

Turn at the Marble Mountain Ski Area sign and follow the road behind the Petro Canada gas station. Follow this road a short distance, but do not cross the small bridge that crosses Steady Brook. Park in the rear parking lot of the Marble Mountain Ski area. Follow the road (marked with two red posts) which gradually starts to climb uphill. This ski area maintenance road switchbacks several times enroute to the top of the chair lift.

Features

Hikers will be rewarded with superb views of the Humber River Valley and as elevation is gained impressive views of the North Arm and Blomidon Mountains are obtained. Some picnic tables are located at various locations enroute.

Length

3.5 kilometres to the top of the chairlift, although good views are obtained well below the summit (one way).

Suitability

Generally easy walking, but with an elevation gain of 1500 feet hikers must be in reasonable condition. In dry summers this trail can be done in running shoes, but hiking boots are recommended if the trail is wet. For the interested hiker a rough trail extends from the top of the chair lift to the summit of Mt. Musgrave, easily identifiable since it has two large boulders near the summit which can be seen from the top of the chairlift. These boulders were probably dropped by glaciers during the last glaciation. This trail is approximately .5 kilometre in length and climbs 200 feet. Although running shoes are adequate from the road to the top of the chairlift, hiking boots are suggested for those people going to the top of Mt. Musgrave.

Topographic Map Reference
Corner Brook 12A/13 (1:50,000)

 ## Cox's Cove to Brake's Cove Trail

Location
Highway 440 winds through many communities along the north shore of the Bay of Islands, the names of which suggest aspects of the origins of the first settlers (Irishtown) or of the favourable climate and soils of this shore (Summerside and Meadows), and ends at Cox's Cove, a small fishing village first settled in the 1840s. Once you reach the water front at Cox's Cove, turn left. The road passes by the fish plant and then climbs slightly before ending. The trail starts next to the guard rail and follows a set of wooden stairs to the beach. Once on the beach, head left along the shore to the abandoned community of Brake's Cove.

Features
This is a scenic coastal walk with interesting sedimentary rock formations along much of the route. Brake's Cove is an abandoned settlement, victim of the Newfoundland government's resettlement program in 1966 when most of the families moved to Cox's Cove. Just ten years prior to this Brake's Cove, with a population of 107 people, was home to eleven families. A cemetary is located at the back of the old community.

Length
1.5 kilometres (one way)

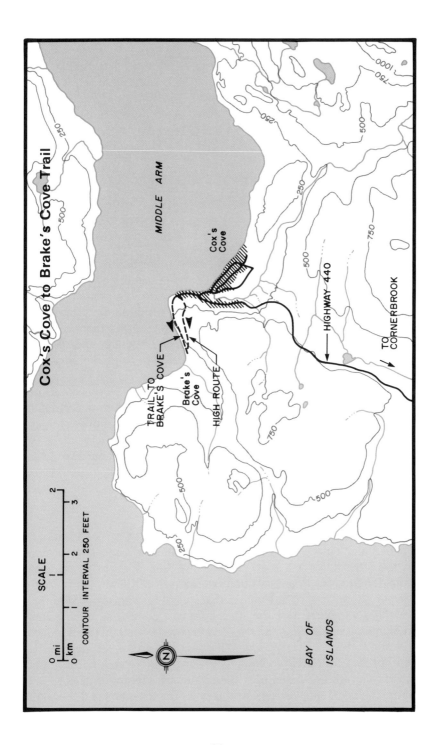

Cox's Cove to Brake's Cove Trail

MIDDLE ARM

Cox's Cove

TRAIL TO BRAKE'S COVE

Brake's Cove

HIGH ROUTE

HIGHWAY 440

TO CORNERBROOK

BAY OF ISLANDS

SCALE

0 mi
0 km

CONTOUR INTERVAL 250 FEET

N

Suitability

This hike is ideal for families since it is short and relatively flat. The coastal route may not be negotiable at high tide, but in this case an alternate inland route over a nearby hill is satisfactory. This alternate route may be wet in places, so rubber or hiking boots may be the preferred footwear if you choose the high route.

Topographic Map Reference

Bay of Islands 12G/1E (1:50,000)

 Blomidon Mountains

The Blomidon Mountains, some of the most interesting and spectacular mountains in Western Newfoundland, provide scenic views of the Bay of Islands. These mountains, which support moderate populations of caribou, moose and ptarmigan, are partially formed from a rare rock called peridotite. From their origins within the earth's mantle, these brown peridotite boulders were pushed to their present position several hundred million years ago when the continents of North America and Africa collided. It is rare to find peridotite at the earth's surface and Western Newfoundland is one of the few places in the world where you can walk on this type of rock. Another noteworthy feature of peridotite is its toxic amounts of some materials, and insufficient quantities of other nutrients, which greatly restricts plant growth. Very few plants have adapted to this bedrock, accounting for it's desert-like appearance. Since much of the terrain is barren or tundra-like, many trips are possible; the following are only suggestions.

Location

Generally, trips into the Blomidon Mountains start at two locations. Routes 1 and 2 (noted on map) start at an unmarked parking lot located on the left side of the road .5 kilometre from the bridge crossing Blomidon Brook. A boardwalk trail extends part of the way along Route 1, a very popular spot in summer that's ideal for families. A side trail (roughly 1 kilometre from the start) goes to a popular swimming area on Blomidon Brook. With the river flowing over smooth bedrock ledges and pools, this very scenic swimming spot is worth a visit even if the weather isn't conducive to swimming. For the more serious hiker, the boardwalk trail continues past the swimming site and begins to cut across the peridotite barrens. At this point the trail ends and the hiker is on his/her own. In this case, follow the general routes presented on the map.

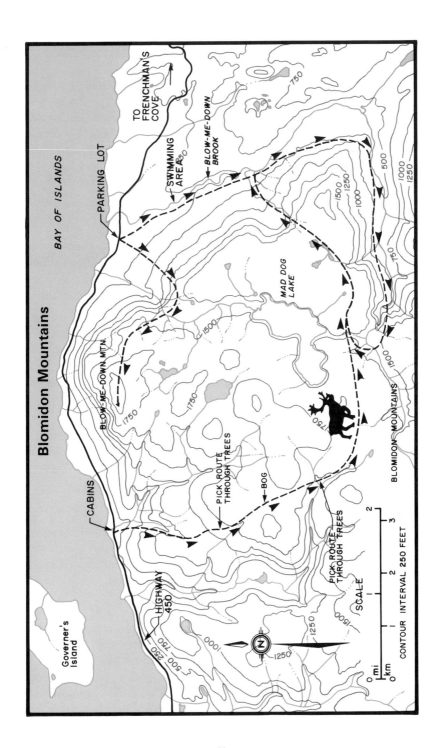

Blomidon Mountains

To complete Route 2, climb up toward the ridge from the parking lot and follow the route indicated on the map.

Route 3 starts at the first collection of fishing cabins, opposite Seal Island (see map). The unmarked trail starts to the left of a small stream that drains the adjacent mountains. It ascends rapidly at first and passes by parts of an old tramway, long dormant mine machinery, and core samples dating from the area's mining heyday between 1871 and 1912. Past the last mine machinery the route is more difficult to follow so a map and compass are suggested for hikers trying to complete Route 3. This route is partially flagged with orange tape.

Features

The highlights of Route 1 are the desert-like peridotite barrens, the Blomidon Brook swimming area, and the possibility of sighting caribou and ptarmigan. As well, the view from the top of the Blomidon Mountains is well worth the effort. Much of the trail is unmarked.

Route 2, which is entirely unmarked, traverses a wide ridge enroute to the summit of Blow-me-down Mountains. From this vantage point views of all parts of the Bay of Islands are spectacular. Again, wildlife sightings are possible. One drawback of the traverse is that once it reaches the ridge, thick vegetation (locally called tuckamore) makes travel difficult. Be prepared to bushwack through certain sections of this route.

Historic mine machinery, likely wildlife (moose and/or caribou) sightings, and good views highlight Route 3. However, this trail is the most difficult of the three hikes, and much of the route is map and compass terrain. Be prepared to bushwack in several places.

Length

Routes 1 and 3 are roughly 16 kilometres; Route 2 is ten kilometres (return). All are one day trips but would make good multi-day adventures as well. Note that Route 3 requires two vehicles or hitchhiking since the trail ends several kilometres from where its starts.

Suitability

The lower portion of Route 1 is designed for families, although it may be wet in places; the swimming area is well worth the walk. Completing all routes requires more stamina and is reserved for more competent hikers. Bring appropriate maps and compass, and wear hiking boots if you intend to complete Route 1 to 3. Because these are unmarked routes with non-existent trails on the barrens and across the tundra, it is suggested that hikers contemplating these routes be experienced in wilderness travel. Tuckamore may make travel difficult and heavy clothing should be worn to protect legs and arms. This latter suggestion is most applicable for Routes 2 and 3.

Topographic Map Reference
Bay of Islands 12G/1E and W (1:50,000)
Serpentine 12B/16E and W (1:50,000)

The Blomidon Mountains provide hikers with rare glimpses of peridotite outcrops (above) and spectacular views of the Bay of Islands (below).

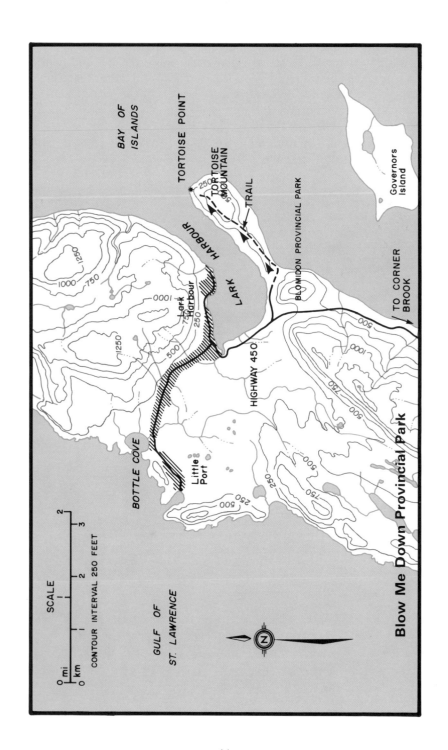

SCALE

0 mi ___1___2___

0 km _1_ _2_ 3

CONTOUR INTERVAL 250 FEET

GULF OF
ST. LAWRENCE

N

BAY OF
ISLANDS

TORTOISE POINT

TORTOISE
MOUNTAIN

TRAIL

BLOMIDON PROVINCIAL PARK

Governors
Island

HARBOUR

LARK

Lark
Harbour

BOTTLE COVE

Little
Port

HIGHWAY 450

TO CORNER
BROOK

Blow Me Down Provincial Park

 **Blow Me Down Provincial Park**

Location

Blow Me Down Provincial Park is located on Highway 450, two kilometres from Lark Harbour (see adjacent map). Visitors to the park are charged a small daily user fee.

Features

A marked and maintained hiking trail leads to a lookout platform, from which one can obtain a panoramic view of the rugged coastline of both York Harbour, Lark Harbour and of the Bay of Islands. A further extension of this trail continues on toward Tortoise Point. Though not maintained, this trail provides inspiring views.

Length

.5 kilometre (one way) to the lookout; roughly 2 kilometres (one way) to Tortoise Point.

Suitability

The lookout trail is ideal for families. Due to the construction of steps, the trail can be easily travelled in running shoes. A side trail leads to the beach via the Governor's Staircase, an interesting return route to the parking lot. The trail beyond the lookout toward Tortoise Point is easy to follow, but not maintained. The occasional deadfall must be negotiated and sturdier footwear is suggested.

Topographic Map Reference

Bay of Islands 12G/IW (1:50,000)

Note

Bottle Cove, at the end of highway 450, also provides a good area for exploring. The Bottle Cove/Little Port area has a long history of settlement. It's first settlers were French who noted its ideal location with respect to passing trading ships and its good access to the nearby fishing grounds. Batteau Cove and Petit Port, as they were once called, changed greatly with resettlement and now have no permanent residents. Although little of historic interest remains, the rugged coastline, secret coves, and wild berries (raspberries and strawberries in season) make this an interesting place to investigate. A day park with washrooms and a sandy beach is also located here.

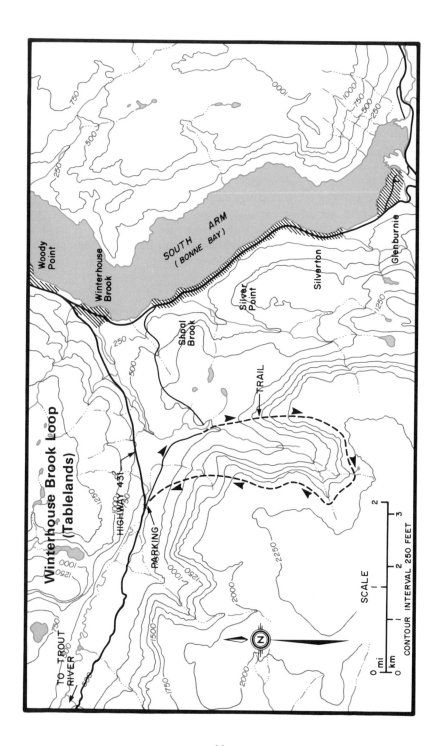

Winterhouse Brook Loop
(Tablelands)

Woody Point

Winterhouse Brook

SOUTH ARM
(BONNE BAY)

Silver Point

Silverton

Glenburnie

Shoal Brook

TRAIL

HIGHWAY 431

PARKING

TO TROUT RIVER

N

SCALE

0 mi
0 km

CONTOUR INTERVAL 250 FEET

Hiking in Gros Morne National Park

The entrance to Gros Morne Park is located on Highway 430, forty kilometres northwest of Deer Lake. Of all the areas of Western Newfoundland, Gros Morne National Park has the best developed hiking trail system. Numerous trails have been built and they are clearly marked and well maintained. A recent addition to the national parks system, Gros Morne has within its boundaries some of the most scenic terrain in Eastern Canada. For the interested backpacker, hiking opportunities range from easy coastal trails to challenging multi-day trips into the rugged Long Range Mountains. As well, a variety of wildlife sightings are probable: moose, caribou, snowshoe or arctic hare, arctic terns, ptarmigan, and possibly whales along the coast.

Combined with striking scenery and wildlife, Gros Morne National Park is also well known for its unique geological attributes. Four hikes are described for the Park area, each highlighting one or more of these wildlife, scenery or geological features. This does not represent a complete listing, but rather illustrates the most interesting and challenging hikes that can be accomplished in the Park. For families interested in shorter hikes, the Park's Visitor's Centre (at Rocky Harbour) can easily supply this information.

 ## Winterhouse Brook Loop (Tablelands)

Location

Turn left on Highway 431 at the community of Wiltondale (40 kilometres from Deer Lake). This road passes by Little Bonne Bay Pond and continues through the small communities of Glenburnie, Birchy Head and Woody Point. Of these communities, Woody Point is the largest and has an interesting heritage. As an historic merchant centre, Woody Point traditionally housed some of the wealthier families in the Bonne Bay region. These homes, with their bay windows, gabled roofs, enclosed porches, and stands of poplar trees, are still in evidence today and make Woody Point's architecture different from that of adjacent communities. Be sure to see Woody Point either before or after a hike on the

Tablelands or the Green Garden Trail. To start the Winterhouse Brook Loop, continue on Highway 431 toward Trout River for a distance of 4 kilometres then turn left into a small parking lot where the hike begins (see map). This route is entirely unmarked.

Features

The Winterhouse Brook Loop has two features which make it a worthwhile hike. Initially the unique geology of this Tablelands region is a fascinating example of the earth's crust in motion, with brown peridotite boulders marking a very unusual time in Newfoundland's geologic history. Several hundred million years ago, when the continents of North America and Africa collided, these boulders were pushed from several miles beneath the ocean floor to their present position atop the Tablelands. This rock, rarely found on the earth's surface today, is toxic to most plants and hence only limited types of specialized vegetation are found in its vicinity. In fact, a view toward Trout River, down Highway 431, will illustrate the dramatic contrast between the forested slopes to the right of the highway and the barren peridotite slopes on the left. One of the few types of vegetation adapted to this environment is the insect-eating pitcher plant, Newfoundland's provincial flower. The other features of this hike are the great views of Winterhouse Gorge, Bonne Bay and Gros Morne Mountain.

Length

10 kilometres (loop)

Suitability

This hike is all on angular rock and so is recommended for competent hikers. An ascent of 1500 vertical feet is required and some scrambling is necessary. Hiking boots with good soles and support are the preferred footwear. Attempt this hike only when the weather is favourable since the route is unmarked and fog could gather quickly obscuring visibility.

Topographic Map Reference

Lomond 12H/5 (1:50,000)

 **Green Garden Trail**

Location

This trail begins roughly 13 kilometres from Woody Point on Highway 431 (toward Trout River). The well-marked trail begins from a large parking lot on the right hand side of the road (see map).

Features

This is a splendid coastal hike, containing some of the most interesting coastline in the Park. Lovely beaches, tall grass meadows, large sea caves, sea stacks and cliffs composed in part of volcanic pillow lavas are some of the attributes that can be found along the rugged coast. While three primitive campsites (with picnic tables and pit toilets) are available for backpackers who wish to overnight, this trip can easily be done in a day. Much of the trail winds along the elevated meadows which fishermen have historically used to pasture their livestock.

Length

The main loop is roughly 20 kilometres return (see map).

Beach campers whale watching on the Green Garden Trail.

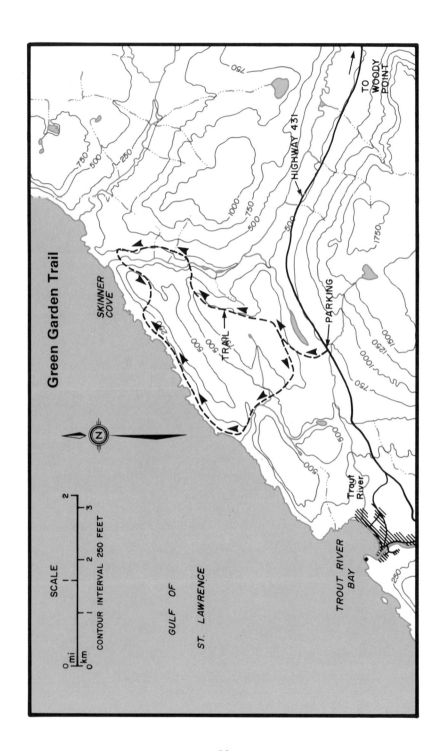

Green Garden Trail

SCALE

CONTOUR INTERVAL 250 FEET

GULF OF

ST. LAWRENCE

SKINNER COVE

TRAIL

TRAIL

HIGHWAY 431

PARKING

TO WOODY POINT

Trout River

TROUT RIVER BAY

Suitability

Considering the length of the trail, this hike is recommended for those in good condition. The trail is well marked and maintained, but read the instructions about boiling water that are posted near the streams. For families or individuals that want a shorter hike to visit this scenic area it is recommended they go as far as the start of the Green Garden overlooking the Gulf of St. Lawrence. Rubber boots or sturdy footwear is recommended.

Topographic Map Reference

Trout River 12G/8 (1:50,000)
Skinner Cove 12G/9 (1:50,000)

 Gros Morne Trail (James Callaghan Trail)

Location

This marked trail is located 3 kilometres south of the Visitor's Centre at Rocky Harbour. For those hikers travelling from Deer Lake, drive north along Highway 430 a distance of 71 kilometres to Rocky Harbour.

Features

This trail was named in honour of former British Prime Minister James Callaghan for his interest in preserving areas of natural beauty. The route winds through spruce and fir of the boreal forest, past bogs and into alpine environments, each home to different animal communities. The observant hiker may see chickadees, warblers, and woodpeckers in the thicker vegetation; a series of beaver ponds are found at the base of the rock gully (the gully marks a gradual change to the alpine environment); and on top caribou, rock ptarmigan and moose may be sited. The 360° view from the top of Gros Morne — Newfoundland's second highest peak — is superb. Be sure to walk along the top of Gros Morne to where the plateau suddenly falls away, dropping 2000 feet to Ten Mile Pond.

Length

11 kilometres (return)

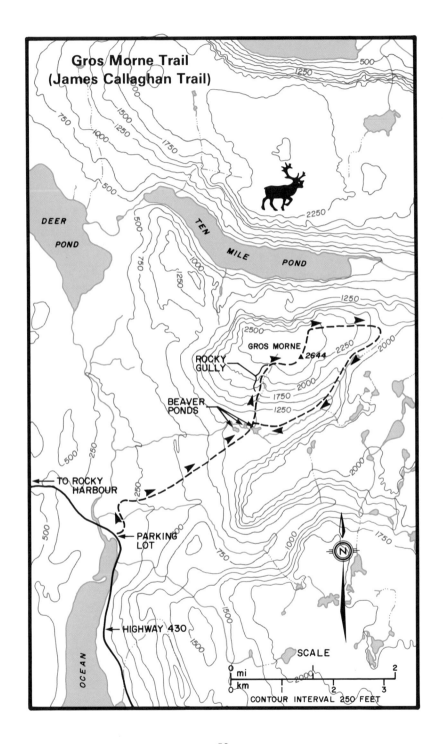

Gros Morne Trail
(James Callaghan Trail)

DEER POND

TEN MILE POND

GROS MORNE
▲2644

ROCKY GULLY

BEAVER PONDS

TO ROCKY HARBOUR

PARKING LOT

HIGHWAY 430

OCEAN

SCALE

mi
km

CONTOUR INTERVAL 250 FEET

Suitability

Because of the steep climb up the rock gully, this hike is recommended for competent and experienced hikers. Although it is not a long hike, it climbs over 2600 feet and hence hikers should be in good physical condition. Due to the elevation gain, wind speeds are often much higher and temperatures much colder on top so dress accordingly. Hiking boots are recommended, and bring water since there is little available along the route. Although the trail is marked by cairns along the summit, be cautious in poor weather since visibility can be quickly reduced in fog. A compass and an actual topographic map are especially useful in these conditions. The indicated route is recommended because of the difficulty descending the rock gully and the interesting terrain covered by the alternate trail around the back. For the families with young children, or people unable to climb the rock gully, a shortened trip to the beaver ponds would be a good day hike.

Topographic Map Reference
Gros Morne 12H/12 (1:50,000)

Long Range Traverse
(Western Brook Pond to Gros Morne)

Location

Drive to the trailhead at the Western Brook Pond parking lot. The first 4 kilometres are on a well maintained trail that leads to the shores of Western Brook Pond. Most people who walk this route do so to take the popular tour boat which travels the length of Western Brook Pond. The remainder of the trail, which starts at the dock at the extreme eastern end of the pond, is unmarked.

Features

This multi-day hike, the longest of those listed in this book, is best suited to experienced backpackers in good physical condition. The highlights include some of the best wilderness hiking in Eastern Canada; almost certain sightings of caribou, ptarmigan and moose; rugged scenery; and a spectacular boat trip that is required to gain access to the trail. This boat trip departs three times a day (weather permitting) and traverses the 16 kilometre length of fjord-like Western Brook Pond. The sheer rock walls, sculpted by glaciers, form spectacular cliffs rising over 2000 feet above the water. The trail passes through many diverse vegetation communities including bog, boreal forest, and alpine ecosystems, by spectacular waterfalls and around numerous scenic lakes.

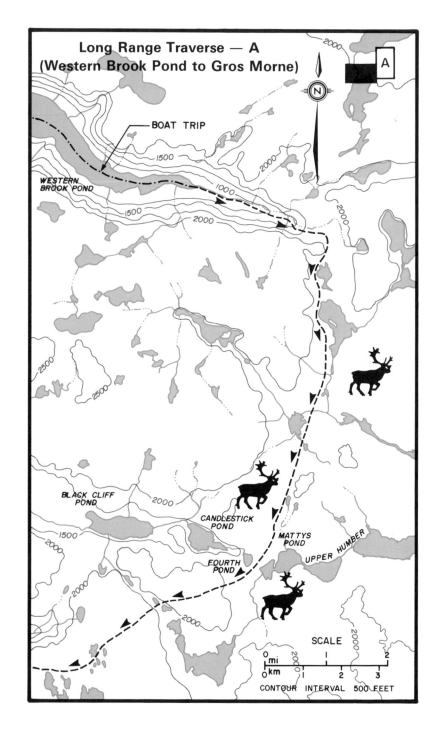

Long Range Traverse — A
(Western Brook Pond to Gros Morne)

A

N

BOAT TRIP

2000

1500

1000

WESTERN
BROOK POND

1500

2000

2000

2500

2500

BLACK CLIFF
POND

2000

CANDLESTICK
POND

MATTYS
POND

UPPER HUMBER

1500

2000

FOURTH
POND

2000

2000

2000

SCALE

0 mi
0 km

1

2

2

3

CONTOUR INTERVAL 500 FEET

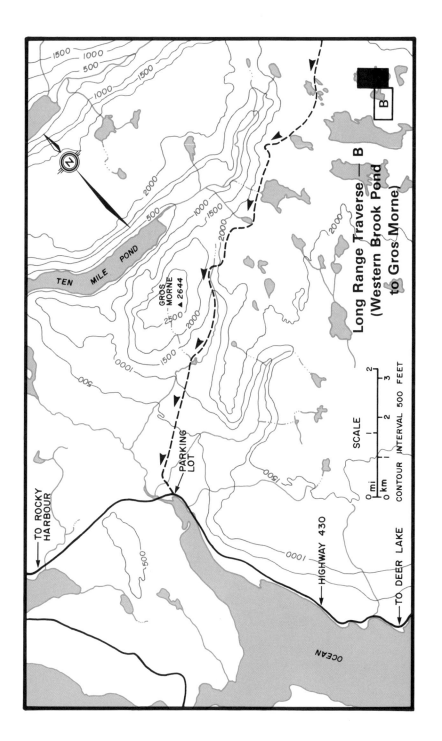

Long Range Traverse — B
(Western Brook Pond to Gros Morne)

TO ROCKY HARBOUR

TO DEER LAKE

HIGHWAY 430

OCEAN

PARKING LOT

GROS MORNE ▲ 2644

TEN MILE POND

SCALE

CONTOUR INTERVAL 500 FEET

55

Length

35 kilometres (including 4 kilometres to Western Brook Pond where the boat trip starts).

Suitability

Except for the initial 4 kilometres to Western Brook Pond, which is well maintained and can be done by hikers of all ages in light footwear, this route is unmarked. Because of the rugged terrain, occasional thick tuckamore, and constant route finding, it is suggested that only groups — a minimum of three hikers is suggested — with considerable hiking experience should plan to start this hike and that at least one member of the group have experience using a map and compass. Although the hike will likely take three to four days to complete, groups should carry provisions for five days, allowing extra time for poor weather which will greatly lessen the distance covered in a day. Allow as well several hours to climb the three to four kilometre gorge at the end of Western Brook Pond. This climb is exhausting and difficult, especially with a full pack. Experience has shown that this traverse shouldn't be underestimated; hikers should be well prepared, particularly in route finding with map and compass. This hike, with its inspiring back country, wild life viewing opportunities and challenging wilderness, is probably unparalleled in Eastern Canada.

Topographic Map Reference

Gros Morne 12H/12 (1:50,000)

Overlooking Ten Mile Pond, with Gros Morne Mountain on the left.

Hiking on the Northern Peninsula

One of the main attractions for most visitors to the Northern Peninsula is the historic Viking settlement at L'Anse aux Meadows, near St. Anthony. This site has been developed by Parks Canada and marks the earliest confirmed evidence of European contact in North America (1000 AD). The United Nations Educational Scientific and Cultural Organization (UNESCO) has labelled the L'Anse aux Meadows area a world heritage site.

Highway 430 stretches 312 kilometres from Rocky Harbour to St. Anthony, winding through several interesting communities enroute. Hawkes Bay is known for its late nineteenth century whaling industry and the remains of the old whaling station are still evident. Port aux Choix is the site of an important archaeological excavation which has uncovered the ancient burial grounds of the Maritime Archaic Indians. A National Historic Park has been developed to interpret these discoveries. Also at Port aux Choix is a superb coastal hike which begins at the Point Riche lighthouse.

It should be noted that, although the Long Range Mountains parallel Highway 430, they are often many kilometres inland. The hikes presented in this short section are, therefore, coastal trails.

 ## Point Riche Lighthouse Trail

Location

The hike starts at the Point Riche Lighthouse located just outside Port aux Choix, several kilometres north of Hawkes Bay off Highway 430.

Features

This coastal trail has two possibilities: one route along the ocean on interesting sedimentary rocks and an alternate higher route along a flattish cliff. The trail over the rocky coastline is not marked but is the most interesting. This coastal route has shore birds, small beaches, tidal pools and hoodoo-like features eroded in the bedrock. The trail along the higher ground is marked by cairns. Both routes end at an outskirt of Port aux Choix.

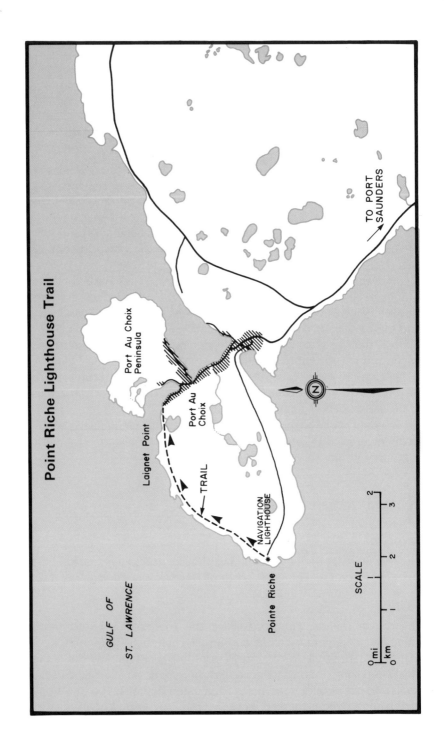

Point Riche Lighthouse Trail

GULF OF
ST. LAWRENCE

Laignet Point

Port Au Choix
Peninsula

Port Au
Choix

TRAIL

NAVIGATION
LIGHTHOUSE

Pointe Riche

TO PORT
SAUNDERS

N

SCALE

0 mi
0 km

58

Length

3.5 kilometres (one way)

Suitability

Since it involves a relatively short distance and has many different features of interest, this route is suited to a variety of hikers. Running or tennis shoes are certainly adequate for this trail. For people planning to hike in both directions, following the coastal route in one direction and the cliff route on the return trip is recommended. The Point Riche lighthouse is also worth visiting.

Topographic Map Reference

Port Saunders 12-I/11 (1:50,000)

Point Riche Trail.

St. Anthony

Originally the French fishing station of St. Antoine settled in the mid 1800s, St. Anthony is today the largest community on the Northern Peninsula. It is situated near L'Anse aux Meadows, the historic Viking settlement site. Although always a fishing community, it is perhaps best known as the base of operations for the medical missionary Dr. Wilfred Grenfell. From a small hospital built there in 1900, Dr. Grenfell travelled extensively along the Labrador coast and throughout Northern Newfoundland bringing medical care to the residents of isolated communities.

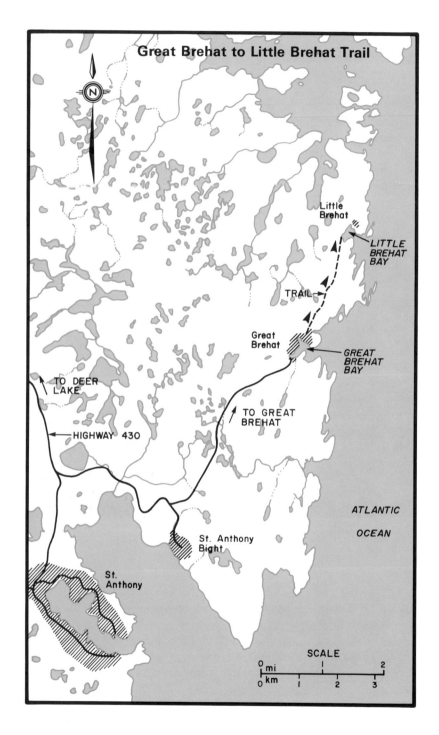

Great Brehat to Little Brehat Trail

N

Little
Brehat

*LITTLE
BREHAT
BAY*

TRAIL →

Great
Brehat

*GREAT
BREHAT
BAY*

TO DEER
LAKE

← HIGHWAY 430

TO GREAT
BREHAT

St. Anthony
Bight

St.
Anthony

ATLANTIC

OCEAN

SCALE

0 mi   1   2
0 km   1   2   3

Great Brehat to Little Brehat Trail

Location

This trail starts from the north end of the community of Great Brehat, just north of St. Anthony Bight, about 7 kilometres from St. Anthony. Ask directions if necessary.

Features

The trail connects the community of Great Brehat to the abandoned community of Little Brehat. Although not much is left of historic interest, the trail winds past small trout ponds and in the fall this area is popular for bakeapples (or cloudberry), a delicious yellow-orange berry. Icebergs are frequently sighted just offshore throughout the summer months.

Length

2.75 kilometres (one way)

Suitability

This short hike is suitable for families, the trail well defined although not officially marked. It may be wet in places so rubber boots are suggested.

Topographic Map Reference

St. Anthony 2M/5 and 2M/6 (1:50,000)

Notes

Notes

Keith Nicol was educated at the University of British Columbia and is now an Assistant Professor of Geography at the Sir Wilfred Grenfell College of Memorial University of Newfoundland. His research and writing interests are varied and include aspects of environmental interpretation and outdoor recreation. Besides being an avid hiker, he enjoys ocean kayaking, canoeing and cross-country skiing.